SPORTS BIOGRAPHIES

NEYMAR

KENNY ABDO

An Imprint of Abdo Zoom
abdopublishing.com

abdopublishing.com

Published by Abdo Zoom, a division of ABDO, P.O. Box 398166, Minneapolis, Minnesota 55439. Copyright © 2019 by Abdo Consulting Group, Inc. International copyrights reserved in all countries. No part of _____ be reproduced in any form without written permission from the pub_____ demark and logo of Abdo Zoom.

Printed in the United States of America, North _____ esota.
052018
092018

Photo Credits: Alamy, AP Images, Icon Sportswire, iStock, Shutterstock
Production Contributors: Kenny Abdo, Jennie Forsberg, Grace Hansen
Design Contributors: Dorothy Toth, Neil Klinepier

Library of Congress Control Number: 2017960659

Publisher's Cataloging-in-Publication Data

Names: Abdo, Kenny, author.
Title: Neymar / by Kenny Abdo.
Description: Minneapolis, Minnesota : Abdo Zoom, 2019. | Series: Sports biographies |
     Includes online resources and index.
Identifiers: ISBN 9781532124808 (lib.bdg.) | ISBN 9781532124945 (ebook) |
     ISBN 9781532125010 (Read-to-me ebook)
Subjects: LCSH: Silva Santos Júnior, Neymar da, 1992-, Biography--
     Juvenile literature. | Soccer players--
     Brazil--Biography--Juvenile literature. | World Cup (Soccer) (2014 : Brazil)-
     Biography--Juvenile literature. | Paris Saint-Germain (Soccer Team)--Biography-
     Juvenile literature.
Classification: DDC 796.334092 [B]--dc23

TABLE OF CONTENTS

NEYMAR

Neymar is a hero to fans of
the Brazil national team. He is
also a star forward on the Paris
Saint-Germain **Club**.

He is known as one of the world's most **prominent** sportsmen. ESPN announced in 2017 that he was the sixth-most famous athlete in the world.

Guyana
Suriname
Venezuela
French Guiana
Brazil
Peru
Bolivia
Chile
Paraguay
MOGI DAS CRUZES
Argentina
Uruguay

Neymar da Silva Santos Jr. was born in Mogi das Cruzes, Brazil, in 1992.

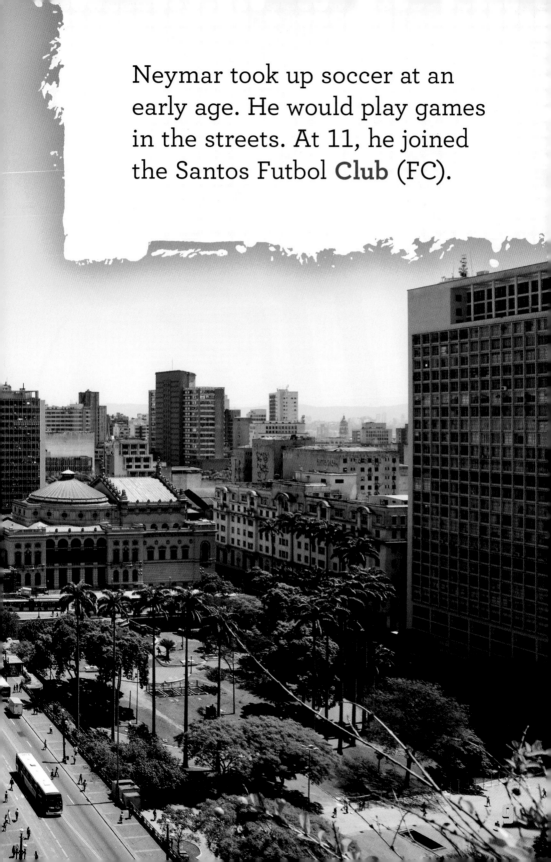

Neymar took up soccer at an early age. He would play games in the streets. At 11, he joined the Santos Futbol **Club** (FC).

Neymar was offered the chance to join Real Madrid at the age of 14. He declined and stayed with Santos FC.

GOING PRO

In 2009, Neymar made
his professional **debut**
with Santos FC. He won
the league's Best Young
Player award that year.

Neymar scored his 100th professional goal on his 20th birthday. He finished the 2012 **season** with an astonishing 43 goals.

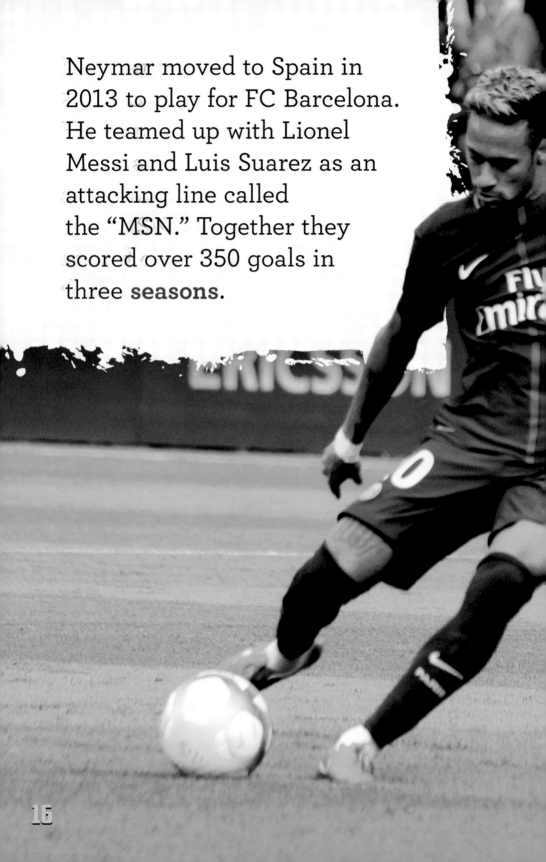

Neymar moved to Spain in 2013 to play for FC Barcelona. He teamed up with Lionel Messi and Luis Suarez as an attacking line called the "MSN." Together they scored over 350 goals in three **seasons**.

Neymar won nine **titles** during his three years with Barcelona.

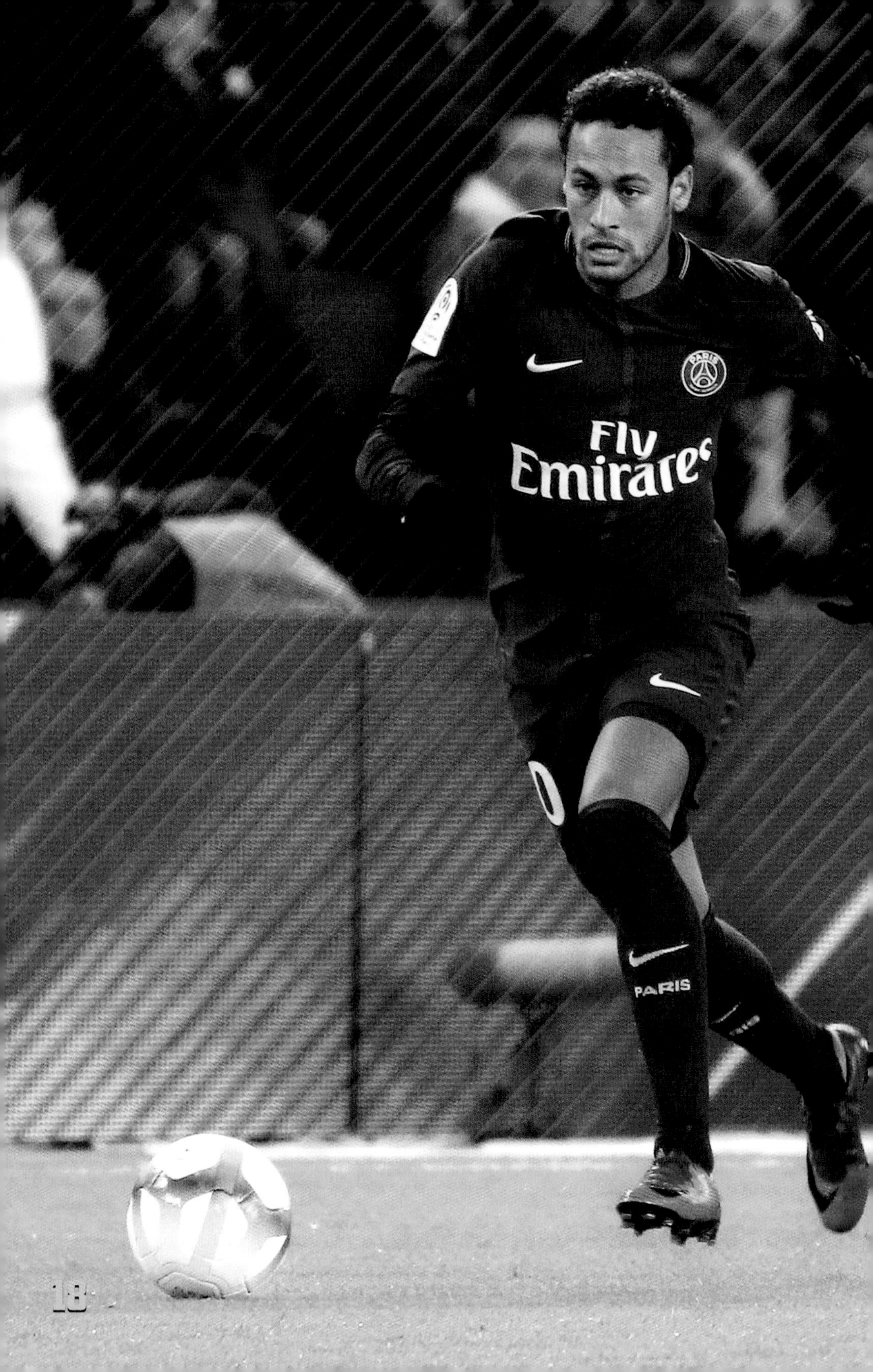
Fly
Emirates
PARIS

In 2017, Neymar left Barcelona to join the French **club** Paris Saint-Germain.

LEGACY

Neymar's yearly **salary** is $53 million dollars. That makes him the highest paid soccer player in the world.

He is the first and only Brazilian athlete to be on the cover of TIME Magazine.

GLOSSARY

club – an association soccer team in a certain league or division.

debut – a first appearance.

prominent – important and famous.

salary – the amount of money you receive for your work.

season – the portion of the year where certain games are played.

title – specifically assigned to a player or team that wins an important soccer competition or event.

ONLINE RESOURCES

Booklinks
NONFICTION NETWORK
FREE! ONLINE NONFICTION RESOURCES

To learn more about Neymar, please visit abdobooklinks.com. These links are routinely monitored and updated to provide the most current information available.

INDEX